COAST
SALISH

Their Art, Culture and Legends

AUTHOR'S NOTE

This little book, although carefully researched, was not especially written for study in anthropological circles. Rather it is intended as light and enjoyable reading to whet the appetite of those who would like to increase their knowledge of a rich way of life which flourished in Coastal British Columbia and the State of Washington before disintregating forces, spearheaded by the coming of non-Indians, swept the old Northwest native cultures away.

Reg Ashwell

COAST SALISH
Their Art, Culture and Legends

by Reg Ashwell

hancock
house

Cataloging in Publication Data

Ashwell, Reg, 1921-
Coast Salish

ISBN 0-88839-009-2

1.   Salish Indians.   2.   Indians of North America
—Northwest coast of North America.
I.   Title.

E99.S2A83   970'.004'97   C78-002069-3

Printed in Hong Kong

Third Printing 1989

Published simultaneously in Canada and the United States by

 HANCOCK HOUSE PUBLISHERS LTD.
19313 Zero Ave., Surrey, B.C. V3S 5J9

HANCOCK HOUSE PUBLISHERS
1431 Harrison Avenue, Blaine, WA 98230

CONTENTS

FOREWORD

"My words are like the stars that never set. . . . Yonder sky, that has wept tears of compassion upon our fathers for centuries untold, and which to us looks eternal, may change. Today it is fair, tomorrow it may be overcast with clouds.

"There was a time when our people covered the whole land as the waves of a wind-ruffled sea covers its shell-paved floor—but that time has long since passed away, with the greatness of tribes almost forgotten.

"Every part of this country is sacred to my people. Every hillside, every valley, every plain and grove, has been hallowed by some fond memory or some sad experience of my tribe.

"Even the rocks, which seem to lie dumb as they swelter in the sun along the silent sea shore in solemn grandeur, thrill with memories of past events connected with the lives of my people.

"The noble braves, fond mothers, glad, happy-hearted maidens, and even the little children, who lived and rejoiced here for a brief season, and whose very names are now forgotten, still love these sombre solitudes and their deep fastnesses which, at even-tide, grow shadowy with the presence of dusky spirits.

"Our dead never forget this beautiful world that gave them being. They still love its winding rivers, its great mountains and its sequestered vales, and they ever yearn in tenderest affection over the lonely-hearted living, and often return to visit, guide, and comfort them."

Extracts from the famous speech by Chief Seattle, the great Suquamish Indian leader.

DONOVAN CLEMSON

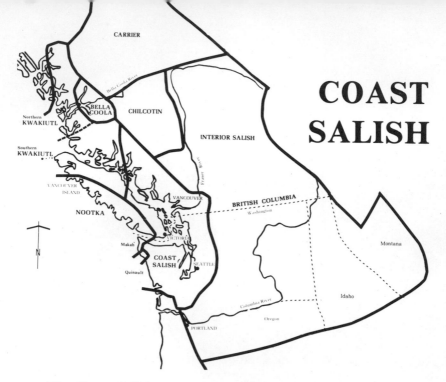

The Coast Salish people are unique among the Indians of the Pacific Northwest. They have in recent times acquired much of the northern native culture, yet they have strong historic connections with the Indians of the Interior. Widely dispersed throughout the Coastal areas of southern British Columbia and the State of Washington, and with footholds far inland along the lower reaches of the Fraser River, the Coast Salish occupied a diversified environment and thus acquired a variety of cultural traits.

The Coast Salish were the most numerous of all the Northwest Coast tribes. In British Columbia alone, the population census of 1835 placed their numbers at 12,000. By 1915, their low year, the usual plagues and diseases brought about by the coming of Europeans had reduced the population to only 4,120. However, there has been a healthy increase in numbers among the Coast Salish in recent years and in 1954 the British Columbia population stood at 6,397 and continues to rise steadily.

The Coast Salish inhabited the coast of the mainland from Bute Inlet in British Columbia to the Columbia River, dividing Washington and Oregon and those areas on Vancouver Island not occupied by the Kwakiutl and the Nootka Indians, from Johnstone Straight to Port San Juan. They also occupied vast areas of western Washington State.

8

Their Origins

There is evidence to suggest that the Coast Salish originally migrated to the Northwest Coast in waves of successive groups, coming from the Interior Plateau on the upper reaches of the Fraser and Thompson Rivers. There are definite language characteristics linking the Coast Salish with their Interior Salish brothers. There are also striking similarities between the artifacts found in Coast shell mounds and those discovered in some of the ancient burial grounds of the more easterly Interior Salish groups.

The early writings of Charles Hill-Tout who, among others, was in close contact with the Salish people in early times before the White occupation brought about the collapse of native cultures, also suggest a strong cultural link between the Coast and Interior Salish people.

Such evidence is strengthened by the several obvious differences which existed between the Coast Salish and other Northwest Coast tribes. Differences in the style of essential tools, such as axes, hammers, etc.; in the construction of their long houses, and in the Coast Salish art forms (which were noticeably much less developed) lead us to the conclusion that the Indians of the Coastal North and the Coast Salish originated from separate cultural backgrounds.

From the pre-historic evidence found in the many shell mounds existing throughout the Coastal area, it may be assumed with reasonable accuracy that the Salish migration to the Pacific Coast took place only a few centuries before the coming of the White man.

We can only imagine what might have caused such a migration over a difficult and dangerous terrain. It may have been a result of one of the endless wars that took place among the many bands that comprised the Interior Salish; or a sudden scarcity of game; or population pressures; or perhaps the haphazardly nomadic wanderings of a few hardy souls.

Whatever the reasons, we can assume that the Salish migration took place in a series of nomadic groups and not as a warlike nation bent on conquering new territory.

And so they came, by-passing the unnavigable waters of the Fraser Canyon—in the vicinity of Lytton and Hope—by crossing the great rugged Coast Range mountains and journeying into a new and beautiful land of gentler climate and teeming with the food resources of the Fraser River Delta and the Coastal waterways.

Did the newcomers migrate to a vast, empty and unoccupied territory? Or did they find a small pre-Salish population, maintaining its own language and culture, yet too few in numbers, or perhaps simply disinclined, to resist the invaders? There are indications that such a population did indeed exist but were eventually absorbed by the Salish who continued to arrive in ever-increasing numbers as word of this new land of plenty spread back to relatives and friends left behind.

Archaeologists dig down through layers of ancient Indian midden remains revealing artifacts of centuries' old occupations.

Coast Salish village, Comox about 1867-70.

If there was a fusion and blending of cultures between the Salish and an older civilization, it may account for the rather noticeable differences in the physical appearance between the Coast Salish and their ancestors from the Interior.

The Coast Salish were usually shorter in stature and less slender than the Interior Indians. Their hair varied from black to a dark, reddish brown. Dark eyes carried little if any of the slightly Oriental slant which so often characterized the Interior and Plains Indians.

From Spuzzum, on the Lower Fraser, the Salish gradually paddled via navigable waters into the Mainland territory around the mouth of the River. Ever following the sea lanes northward, they eventually reached as far as Bute Inlet. Finally they occupied the San Juan and Gulf Islands and parts of Vancouver Island, penetrating north as far as the Salmon River.

The newcomers must indeed have thought, as they traveled ever westward via the waterways to the Pacific Coast, that they had reached a land of milk and honey—a veritable Temlaham (Paradise) —the Gitksan garden of Eden of which Barbeau wrote so dramatically in his "Downfall of Temlaham"; a land very different from the country they had left behind, with its hot short summers followed by long, bitterly cold winters.

11

The Land

The Coastal wilderness.

    Here was a new land of dense forests with a heavy growth of fir, cedar, spruce, hemlock and pine. Due to the prevailing moist climate, the evergreens reached awesome heights and the heavy undergrowth caused much of the great forested areas to become all but impenetrable by land.

    North to Bute Inlet, which was the most northerly extent of Coast Salish settlement, the heavily timbered, mountainous terrain of the Interior extends to the very edge of a deeply indented shoreline. In the Coastal areas the winters are mild with many sunless days of mist and rain. Further inland, in the river valleys, an easier topography prevails. The giant evergreens are replaced by birch, alder, poplar, maple and willow trees. Here the climate is more extreme and snow accumulation in the uplands is greater.

12

HOUSES

To the Salish people, migrating from harsher climes, this new land must have appeared as a paradise of great natural wealth. Wealth to them, of course, had nothing to do with precious metals or stones, such as gold and silver or diamonds and rubies. The wealth lay in the teeming supplies of natural food resources. There were fish in plenty in the rivers and streams and in the open sea; game abounded in the forests, and in the more open areas wild berries grew in profusion and bulbs and roots could be dug from the rich soil with relative ease.

The great stands of tall, straight red cedar trees were eminently suitable for the building of communal style dwellings and the Coast Salish constructed huge, grandly spacious houses, far removed from the almost subterranean, dark and airless structures built as permanent winter homes in their ancestral homeland among the Interior Salish. The kekuli (semi-subterranean houses) were occasionally built by the Coast Salish in early times and examples of them have been recorded at Point Grey, Howe Sound, and Bute Inlet.

From the red cedar, Coast Salish men hollowed out their dugout canoes and carved the masks for their Shamanistic rituals and Ceremonial Dances. In later years, under the cultural influences of the Kwakiutl and other Northwest Coast tribes, the Coast Salish carved inside house-posts for their long houses. Grave figures were also noted by the fur traders and early explorers.

Again from the prized cedar tree, the women stripped the bark, and they were always careful not to injure or kill the tree by taking too much bark at one time. The precious bark was put to innumerable uses, including the weaving of short, fringed skirts for everyday wear and the making of fine baskets which were used essentially as containers during the gathering of berries, roots, bulbs, clams, and other necessities of life.

The importance of the western red cedar to the Indian tribes of the Northwest Coast cannot be over emphasized, especially in the pre-European era, before the use of iron and steel, when the native people used only stone tools for carpentry work involved in the building of the long houses, the hollowing out of canoes, and the making of wooden containers, such as buckets and storage boxes. It was the relatively soft wood of the cedar which made carpentry with

13

Inside and outside
house poles.

stone tools possible. The wood is so straight-grained it can be split
into sections with stone or even elkhorn wedges. In older times,
before intensive logging, the mighty cedar trees—growing on the
coastal strip from Northern California to Southern Alaska—
towered as high as two hundred feet. Most of the great trees have
been cut down now, but you can still see the stumps, sometimes
measuring six or more feet across.

Early pioneers arriving in Northwest Coast harbors, were
amazed at the size of the huge wooden plank houses lining the
shores. Made by people who knew only stone hammers and wedges
of wood or horn, they were incredible structures.

The Coast Salish houses in particular sometimes reached
extreme proportions in size. The great Chief Seattle (Sealthh), after
whom the City of Seattle was named, owned a house one hundred
feet long and holding ten families. His brother built a special feast
house five hundred and forty feet long. And according to an account
by the famous explorer Simon Fraser (for whom the Fraser River
was named), he once entered a Chief's house which measured six
hundred and forty feet in length by sixty feet broad! All of the
interior apartments are described as being square except the Chief's,
which was ninety feet long. The houses were not always this large,
and indeed the lodges of the common people would be considcrably
smaller.

14

The Coast Salish houses were usually built in a shed type style, with the flat roofs gently pitched because of the great width of the structures, inclining upward from front to rear. The Coast Salish found these roofs very useful for drying fish and they also used them as handy platforms for viewing the Potlatches and other ceremonial gatherings and festivities! Moreover, the sloping roofs were advantageous in shedding rain. By grooving the wide cedar boards of the roof lengthwise in a flat U shape, and then arranging them alternately so that the flange of one board was turned down to fit into the upturned flange of the next, the rain was diverted into a series of channels and carried to the lower edge of the roof.

The roofs of the long houses were supported by a heavy individual framework independent of the walls. There were two basic methods employed in putting on the wall planks. They could be placed horizontally, one above the other, and tied to the framework, or to extra upright posts, by cedar withes. But the most usual, and certainly the simplest method, was to place the wall boards upright and hold them vertically by driving their ends deep into the earth.

Cracks in the walls were sometimes chinked with moss and usually they were covered on the inside with mats. But the cracks were useful in that they kept a good circulation of air in the house and allowed the escape of any residue of smoke from the lodge fires that had not found its way through the holes in the roof which were left for that purpose.

Salish house at Comox.

15

The floors of these great long houses were usually of earth, sometimes dug down but usually left at ground level. Some families sprinkled the earth with sand. Others laid down hand woven mats for use as a carpet. In the house of a wealthy Chief the floor might be covered with planks.

Inside a northern (Bella Coola) house which shows construction. Sleeping platforms were often larger than shown.

Dug into the floors were shallow pits for fireplaces and these pits were often walled with stones or heavy timbers to prevent the fires from spreading. The number of the fire pits depended on the size of the house. A two family house was one large room, with a fire pit at each end. Four family houses had a fire close to each corner. The really large houses, such as Chief's houses, were divided up into compartments, each with its own fire. These compartments, occupying the space between two uprights, were usually about ten or twelve feet wide. The walls were often made by standing vertical planks on the earthen floor, with their tops resting against the cross beams. Alternately, if the planks were scarce, rush mats could be hung from the cross beams.

16

Since the Coast Salish knew nothing of glass before the coming of Europeans, their houses boasted no windows, although the larger houses had several doors. Even the smaller houses had at least two doors, one at the front to be used as an entrance and an "escape" door, most likely placed on a side of the house facing the forest. The doors were covered with a curtain of deer or elk skins. If it were felt there existed a danger of enemy attack, planks were piled up from inside against the openings. In the case of some Coast Salish bands, such as the Quinault, the front or main door was an oval opening, raised about three feet from the ground. The door was just large enough for an adult to squeeze through—a deliberate arrangement planned so that an enemy who was rash enough to attempt an entry found it a slow procedure, and could be quickly overcome by the watchful occupants, armed with clubs and poised to attack him.

Indeed, the long house was at all times an important fortification against enemy attack, with the stout cedar planks providing protection for the occupants, who vigorously directed their arrows through crevices in the walls, often with telling effect.

Coast Salish houses contained little in the way of furniture. Raised sleeping platforms, about four feet (120 centimetres) wide and approximately the same distance from the ground, were built around three walls. In front of them, other platforms were built for use as seats, about two feet (60 centimetres) high and also useful as a step up to the sleeping quarters.

Great drying racks, supported by the cross beams, and used especially for drying salmon, were an ever-present necessity in the long houses. High shelves were often built around the space under the roof slope, where there was always a good circulation of air.

West Coast Nootka house as depicted by early explorers.

17

These shelves made excellent storage spaces for dried clams and other food supplies which rotted easily. Holes were also dug in the ground, below the bunk or seats, where additional food could be stored at a reasonable temperature. Storage boxes and baskets were packed tightly on platforms and seats not used for sitting or sleeping and even placed on extra shelves slung from the cross beams.

The interior of the Coast Salish long house was remarkably tidy and cozy looking. The sleeping platforms, with their bedding of fur robes and bird skins, looked comfortable and inviting. The multi-purpose rush mats were everywhere.They were used as carpets on the floor and as spreads on the bunks. They hung as partitions, or over shelves, and often covered some of the wall cracks. Clean ones were always kept handy for a guest to sit on or to be used as table mats. Items kept on the floor, such as cooking stones and storage boxes, were arranged in as neat and orderly a fashion as possible.

Sometimes the Coast Salish men built a work shed outside the long house and retired there to make their adzes and hammers, or perhaps to carve a mask, ladle or bowl, while the women-folk carried on with their cooking and other chores like making new rush mats, or weaving the famous Salish blankets.

Not all Coast Salish long houses were of the shed type, with long, gently sloping roofs. The Sechelt band, for example, strongly influenced by their northern neighbors the Kwakiutl, built their long houses in the Kwakiutl style, utilizing a gabled roof.

Frame for northern style gabled roof house.

E.S. CURTIS

Temporary summer
shelter of mats.

During the summer months, the Coast Salish all but abandoned their winter long houses and journeyed away on prolonged camping trips, returning for a week or two and staying just long enough to organize themselves for another trip. The reasons for these journeys were many and varied. Food had to be gathered and stored for the winter months ahead. This involved land hunting and fishing for the men and related work for the women, who fitted their work to suit their husband's activities, utilizing days when they were not needed for the process of meat or fish drying.

While the men fished, the women dug for shellfish and gathered clams; or during inland hunting trips, while the men went after game, the women picked berries or dug for roots and bulbs. Children of course, accompanied their elders and assisted in the work as an essential part of their training. During these nomadic months, they lived in the open or under temporary make-shift shelters.

Summer encampment at Comox. 19

MUS. MAN. NAT. MUS. CAN.

TRADE

MUS. MAN. NAT. MUS. CAN.

Indians camped around White settlements to facilitate trading.

Like all the Indians of the Pacific Northwest and indeed, throughout the Americas, the Coast Salish traded with well-established values being calculated in shells, including the coveted abalone shell, coppers, slaves, hides, ivory, basketry, blankets, and various forms of art work. Neighboring bands, such as the Songhees of Vancouver Island and Klallum of Washington, traded extensively with each other. With the coming of the White man, trade became intensified for many years.

With the arrival of the Russians in Alaska and new trade areas opening with the newly horse-mounted Indians of the dry interior country east of them, Northwest Coast tribes became extensively exposed to new ideas. They even traded occasionally for the feathered war bonnets of the Plains and Kootenay Indians, admiring such finery without much need or use for it, yet taking great delight in the rows of Eagle feathers with their quill worked head-bands.

With the advent of White trading posts east of the Rockies and the coming of the Russians to Alaska, Northwest Coast tribes became aware of beautiful colors which before had been only visually apparent in the form of sunsets over still waters or perhaps the reds and golds of autumn leaves. In exchange for the gorgeous robes of animal furs which the Indians wore so casually in cold weather, the Hudson's Bay trading companies and the Russian traders were eager to exchange colored glass beads and ornaments dear to the Indian's heart.

20

CLOTHING

Chief Simon Baker of Capilano Band
wearing ceremonial costume.

In those days Venice was renowned as the glass center of the world. White traders, quickly aware of the Indians' love of color, bought glass beads and baubles from Venice and the far east.

The Indians of the Northwest Coast, not appreciating at first the huge discrepancies in values, which weighed heavily in favor of the greedy traders, eagerly traded their priceless fur pelts for the glass beads, radiant as they were in colors the natives had only seen in a bird's plumage. Now their own beads and shell ornaments of brown and white could be augmented or replaced by beautiful glass beads from far off lands.

The hexagons in rich blues, brought by the Russians from Venice, were particularly popular and have been found in Indian graves—silent proof of the esteem in which these colorful baubles were held by their owners. Today the old trade beads have a new value; they have become highly collectible and much sought after for their historic significance.

Exciting metals such as brass, silver and copper, were also available from the traders. Coast Salish women historically tied sinews around their ankles for a beautifying effect. Now they could replace these with shiny copper anklets, some of the ladies mounting five or six on one ankle!

21

The Northwest Coast Indians were a creative and artistic people, innovative and eager to experiment with new ideas. Soon the more northerly tribes—the Tlingit, Haida, Tsimshian, and Kwakiutl Indians—began making their own style metal ornaments. Silver dollars were beaten down and shaped and engraved to make beautiful bracelets, pendants, and brooches with exciting Northwest Coast designs depicting Beaver, Bear, Killer Whale, Shark, Raven, and Eagle, to mention but a few. They were eagerly sought after up and down the coast and worn with great pride by the wealthy classes.

Among the Coast Salish, as indeed among all the tribes of the Pacific Northwest, clothing styles were the last to change. But with the opening of a Hudson's Bay trading post at Vancouver, near Portland, in 1826 and the subsequent appearance of the famous Hudson's Bay blankets, the old styles gave way to different modes of dress.

The rifle replaced the bow and arrow and spear, making it easier and faster to slaughter the fur bearing animals. Stone tools gave way to iron hammers and steel bladed knives. Wooden receptacles, such as bowls for holding fish oil and ladles made of alder, yew or maple, and of course the incredible storage boxes, which were produced by steaming the soft cedar, bending it into shape, and then lacing the single join with twisted cedar rope, all these passed into an unfortunate obsolescence as the native people became more dependent on the manufactured hardware and other goods so easily obtainable at the trade store.

The traders were eager for the fabulously profitable fur pelts and in order to obtain the goods they desired, the Coast Salish and other Northwest Coast tribes abandoned age old beliefs which forbade the killing of wildlife except for the immediate necessities of life, and aided in the wholesale slaughter of fur bearing animals. Most sought after of all were the soft, glossy pelts of the Sea Otter and as a result these beautiful, intelligent little mammals were exterminated along the British Columbia and Washington Coasts by the early 1900's despite last minute efforts to save them.

The fur traders of those early days got along well with their Indian brothers and did not consciously attempt to interfere with native life styles. But changes resulting from white contact were inevitable. Furs the Salish once used for cloaks went into the Hudson's Bay store houses and the Salish replaced them with store bought woolen blankets, most of them a drab grey in color.

Traditional garments of woven grasses
and cedar bark quickly gave way to
trade goods clothing.

Yet it was not until after white settlers began to arrive in numbers and missionaries were sent in among the native peoples that drastic changes came about.

The Coast Salish were among the first of the Northwest Coast Indians to be seriously affected by the new white authority. Vancouver Island and British Columbia became British Crown Colonies and Governor Sir James Douglas lost no time in establishing British authority over the native people. Missionaries, determined to spread out among the Indians and Christianize them, were given the power of magistrates and Indians who seriously opposed the new regime could be thrown in jail.

One thing the newcomers would not tolerate was the Indian habit of going around in a state of near or total nudity. In those days, pioneer women wore long skirts down to their ankles and it was considered downright sinful to be seen in public without some sort of modestly suitable attire. The Coast Salish, among other tribes, were warned against being seen by the Whites unless dressed to standards acceptable in the Victorian era.

So the Indians obligingly changed and they have been wearing White man's style clothing for about 125 years, except for special ceremonial occasions, when sometimes old costumes—or copies of old costumes—are worn.

Yet clothing styles among the Indians of the Pacific Northwest were extremely practical, and it was unfortunate for them that at that time non-Indians thought it right and necessary to cover their

23

Cedar bark cape is worn by lady preparing more cedar bark by beating it to soft pliable strands.

Note tump line across forehead to support weight of baskets heavy with clams.

Dominic Charlie (right) and his dance group teach traditional
dances. Cultus Lake, 1968.

bodies with layers of heavy clothing.

Coast Salish women wore a fringed skirt of shredded cedar
bark or of rushes fastened at the waist. The men very often wore
nothing at all. In rainy weather, capes of cedar bark or rushes were
worn, their smooth woven surfaces being ideal for shedding the
water. Inside the houses, the capes were removed so that the wearers
did not catch cold in their wet garments.

But woven capes of cattails and cedar bark were not sufficient
covering during the long cold winters, especially for the upriver
Salish, who lived in a land of easier topography. There the dense
forests of giant evergreens were usurped by such trees as birch,
willow, alder and maple. The wet, foggy and near sunless days of the
long winters of the Coastal areas were frequently supplanted by
heavy snows and bitter cold.

The Coast Salish fashioned cold weather robes for themselves
from almost any skin of bird or beast. According to early accounts,
when the Indians boarded the ships of early explorers, wearing their
beautiful mantles of Sea Otter, Martin, and Lynx, the white men
were amazed at the beauty of the many fine pelts and quick to realize
the wealth to be attained in trade for the valuable furs.

Coast Salish women prepared the furs by scraping the insides
and rubbing them with animal brains kept for the purpose. Large
skins, such as bear skins, could be worn whole. Sea Otter pelts were
smaller and five or six had to be sewn together. This was
accomplished by making holes with bone awls, and drawing thin
strips of skin through them in rough stitches.

Leggings and moccasins were not popular with the Coast
Salish, who usually preferred to go barefoot. The moist climate of
the Coastal areas was not suitable for buckskin footwear because
the wet leather first leaked and then dried out as stiff as a board.

25

BEAUTY CARE

A myth has been perpetuated that the North American Indian was dirty and careless about his appearance. The complete opposite was the case and the Coast Salish Indians, being a people who lived on the waterways and the seashore, had plenty of water to wash in and they were in the habit of bathing every morning as soon as they arose. They made their own soap by boiling down thimbleberry bark and by other means such as bruising the leaves of the fragrant mock orange shrub to a soapy lather. After really dirty work, like digging in the ground for roots and bulbs or handling fish and game, they scoured themselves with cedar branches.

The Coast Salish were by necessity an outdoors people and their skins, which were a shade lighter than many tribes, glowed with health and vitality and were remarkably free from the blemishes and pimples which have plagued white people especially in adolescence. During the pre-white era, the Indians enjoyed a balanced diet, free from an over-abundance of starch and sugar and the results were apparent in healthy, glowing skin and strong white teeth. It has been recorded that the Nootkan Indians, seeing White men for the first time after Cook's landing at Friendly cove, were shocked by the sight of the broken, yellow teeth of the sailors and repelled by the odor of stale perspiration from the sailors' sweating unwashed bodies.

Abalone ear ornaments were popular then as now.

E.S. CURTIS

The heads of babies were bound to force skull into sloping back—a sign of beauty to several Northwest Coast tribes.

The representative Coast Salish man was broad shouldered and sturdy, sometimes sporting a little beard and a moustache. Utilizing the two halves of a clamshell, he plucked his eyebrows into a fine line and kept his beard trimmed and tidy.

The Coast Salish, like other Northwest Coast Indian tribes, had strong and definite ideals of beauty care. Tiny babies had their limbs constantly rubbed to keep them straight; the little noses were pinched to make them high and thin and the ears encouraged to lay flat and close to the head. A flattened forehead, with the head sloping upward to the crown, was considered a mark of beauty. A pad, usually of cedarbark, was attached to the baby's cradle and bound against the forehead. By slow pressure, over a period of time, the forehead was gradually flattened to the shape preferred.

Indian maidens dieted for ceremonial purposes, but also to keep themselves slim, youthful and aristocratic looking. Women of the Quilleute band used a sunburn lotion of sea lettuce. Klallam girls ate rose hips for a sweet breath and Lummi maidens rubbed their bodies with the bedstraw plant to give themselves a sweet aromatic odor of perfume.

27

FOOD

Salmon

Nature set a bountiful table for the Coast Salish, as indeed for all of the Northwest Coast tribes. Salmon were by far the most important source of food, and were as basic a food to the Coast Salish as is bread to the White man. According to Indian legend the salmon were not really fish at all but people, living in a great magic wooden house under the sea. Every summer they sent their young men and women, disguised as fish, to meet the native people and to provide their food. When a salmon was caught and eaten, it immediately took form again in the home village.

To the Coast Salish, the coming of the first spring salmon was the most important event in the year. The salmon must be treated with proper respect, and each Indian band had its own ceremony for cleaning and cooking the fish, based on age old directions given by the salmon people themselves.

According to Indian belief, there were five tribes of salmon, all living in a great long house under the sea. White people also know these five "tribes" under their own scientific names—Chinook (spring), Sockeye (red), Coho (silver), Humpback (pink), and Dog (chum). Each salmon "tribe" had its own breeding places and habits and these behavioral patterns were as familiar to the native people as the coming of the seasons.

The coming of the first spring salmon was treated as a very important event, since the Indians believed him to be the scout for the entire salmon village and if he was not treated properly the salmon people might be offended and decide to stay away. The man who caught him treated him almost reverently, laying him down carefully with his head upstream, so that the run would follow. Then he took the salmon home to his wife and summoned the village.

The weir at top contains a salmon trap—when enough fish are caught some woven panels are removed to let fish upstream. Bottom weir just blocks fish migration so they can be easily speared. Cowichan River, 1973.

Net slung into turbulent waters to intercept fish on Fraser River.

Dipnetting milling fish.

Drying salmon.

Jigs

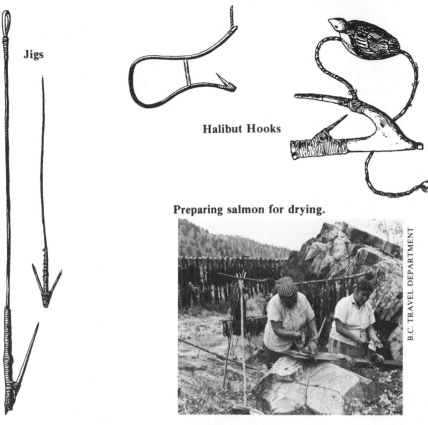

Halibut Hooks

Preparing salmon for drying.

Salmon caches on Fraser River—where dried salmon are stored.　　31

A First Salmon ceremony followed in which rigid rules of procedure were followed. The fish must be cleaned with fern leaves; it must be cut with an ancient knife of stone or mussel shell, with the cuts made up and down, not crosswise. The fish was usually cut down the backbone, which was removed, with the head on it, and the fish opened out. Then short sticks were placed across it to stretch it flat and it was roasted on a split stick before the fire. Sometimes the salmon was broken up with the hands and then boiled. The ritual included taking a piece of this first salmon and finishing eating it before sundown.

After the ceremonies in the villages were over, and the run really began, everyone worked hard to harvest the salmon. While the men and boys fished and gathered wood, the women were kept busy drying the fish on long frames over smoking fires.

The fish were caught with traps, spears and nets, with each village studying its own stream and using the devices best suited to that kind of water, whether shallow or deep, swirling or clear.

If a stream was shallow and clear, a favorite method was to build a weir or fence clear across it. The men stood on platforms along the top of the weir and scooped up the fish with long handled nets as they swarmed against the obstruction.

After the salmon was thoroughly smoked and dried, a long and tedious process, it was carefully stored away in bales or in the woven baskets native women made for the purpose.

The salmon, along with the many other varieties of fish found in both fresh water and salt, formed the basis of the Indians' diet.

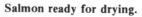

Salmon ready for drying.

COAST SALISH

Simon Charlie and mask.

SIMON CHARLIE CARVINGS

Simon Charlie of Koksilah is one of the master carvers who restimulated interest in traditional Coast Salish carving. His bold images reflect the traditional figurine quality of Salish art.

Bear crest

Simon Charlie pole depicting eagle and bear-mother story.

Dog fish mask
by J. Johnny

Many modern Salish carvers
are incorporating northern style
design with traditional styling
to produce very exciting items.

Halibut-man pole
by Wilber Canute

Talking stick—Cicero August

Frances Horn wolf bowl—a modern stylization.

Man with copper—

Frog rattle—

DOUG LA FORTUNE
CARVINGS

Sea Otter bowl—

Frog Bowl—

Seal bowl

Wind Mask

Moon Mask

FLOYD JOSEPH CARVINGS

Sealion bowl

Eagle-raven-hawk bowl

Floyd Joseph at work on loon bowl.

FLOYD JOSEPH CARVINGS

Floyd Joseph, now of Victoria, at 24 is one of the most talented Salish artists though his distinctive works reflect the Northwest Coast form as opposed to strictly Salish elements.

Gamblers mask

Hawk mask

Dominic Charlie

Carding wool

Salish leaders are rekindling interest in dancing, weaving and basketry.

Knitting Cowichan sweaters is recent

Weaver and basket maker are from Chilliwack

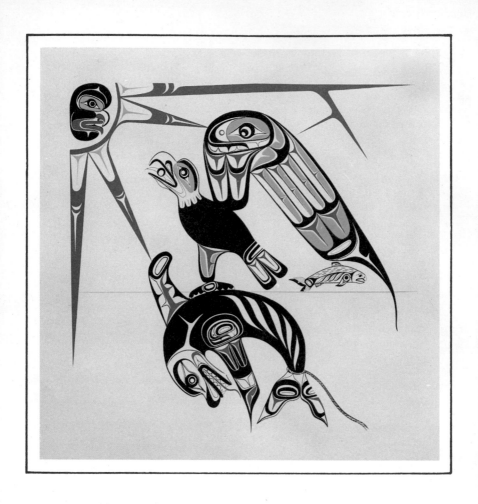

Legend as told and illustrated by Floyd Joseph.

     Reproduced from an original drawing by Floyd Joseph. This drawing represents an illustration of an ancient Squamish legend—"Why the Salmon came to Squamish waters." It all happened a long time ago, when animals and birds and people were really the same, only disguised in different forms. The Chief of the Squamish band was sad because no Salmon lived in Squamish waters and sometimes the people went hungry. One day the village was visited by four brothers who were possessed of great supernatural powers. The sorrowing Chief decided to ask the brothers for help in persuading the Salmon People to swim to Squamish shores.

The four brothers, who were famous for their good deeds, gladly offered their services. But a problem presented itself. Where did the Salmon People live? How could they be found? It was decided to ask Snookum the Sun. Snookum could see all over the world from his home in the sky. But how could anyone get near enough to Snookum to ask him anything? Obviously the Sun would have to be tricked into coming down to the Squamish village.

After much pondering of the matter and discussion the brothers used their great powers and the youngest of them was transformed into a Salmon and then tied to the shore with a fishing line. The Salmon leaped and sported in the water until he attracted the attention of Snookum. But before doing anything the crafty Sun caused the three brothers to go into a deep trance. Then, having changed himself into the form of a magnificent Eagle, Snookum flew down from the sky, dug his claws into the Salmon, and rose rapidly up into the heavens, breaking the line in his flight.

But the brothers, upon waking from their trance, decided to try again. This time they transformed the third brother into a Whale and then tied him to the shore with a very strong line. For the second time Snookum cast the brothers into a trance and descended from the sky in the form of an Eagle. He landed on the floating Whale and dug his claws into the flesh. At first it seemed the great Sun-Eagle would surely lift the Whale right out of the water. But the rope did not break and the frantic flapping of the Eagle's wings did not succeed in freeing his claws from the back of the Whale.

While the struggle continued, the brothers awoke from their trance. The Whale was pulled into shore, the captured Eagle still on his back. Thoroughly outwitted, Sun-Eagle agreed to tell the brothers the whereabouts of the home of the Salmon people in exchange for his release.

Snookum revealed that the Salmon people lived a long distance away to the west but cautioned that if the Squamish people desired to visit with them they must first prepare much medicine and take it with them on the journey. The Sun was then allowed to go and—still in his Eagle form—he took flight and soared away and up into the clouds back to his home in the sky.

Led by the brothers, the Squamish people paddled in their canoes, traveling ever westward, until they reached the home of the Salmon, where they were very cordially received. The Squamish gave some of their mèdicine to Spring Salmon, the Chief of the village, and as a result of this he was very friendly to the whole party.

In a stream which flowed behind the village, Spring Salmon kept a fish trap. The Salmon Chief directed four of his young people, two boys and two girls, to enter the water and swim up the creek into the Salmon-trap. Obeying his orders the young people drew their blankets up over their heads and walked into the sea. No sooner had the water lapped against their faces than they became Salmon. Leaping and playing together, just as Salmon do in the running season, they swam their way to the trap in the creek.

Later, when it came time to welcome the strangers with a feast, Spring Salmon ordered the fish to be brought from the trap to be cleaned and roasted. The four salmon were cleaned and cut open and then spread above the flames on a wooden grill.

When the Chief invited his guests to eat he made a point of insisting that they must not throw away any of the bones. They were to lay them aside carefully, taking care that not even a small bone was destroyed. When the meal was over and the satisfied guests had finished eating, all the bones were carefully gathered up and thrown into the sea. A few minutes later, the four young people who had earlier entered the sea and been changed into salmon, re-appeared in their original human form and waded out of the water to join the others. As a result of this strange occurrence and similar happenings, such as the time a curious guest held back some of the bones at a later feast, the Squamish became convinced that they had indeed found the home of the Salmon people. This withholding of some of the bones resulted in a near disaster, with one of the youths coming out of the sea with part of his face missing and being made whole again only when the guilty Squamish youth produced the bones, pretending he had just found them.

The eldest of the four brothers explained the purpose of their visit to the Salmon Chief. He told how the Squamish people were often poor and hungry, and requested that Salmon be allowed to visit Squamish waters and swim in the Squamish streams.

Chief Kos (Spring Salmon) agreed on one condition. The condition was that the Squamish be very careful with the bones and always be sure to throw them back in the water, just as they had seen the Salmon people do.

"If you are careful with the bones," said Chief Kos, "My people can return to us again after they visit you."

The four brothers and the Squamish people promised to adhere carefully to this rule, thanked their host, and prepared for their return journey across the water, toward the rising sun.

As they were leaving, Chief Kos called to them: "I will send Spring Salmon to you first in the season. After them I will send the Sockeye, then the Cohoe, then the Dog-Salmon, and last of all the Humpback."

The Chief kept his word and ever since that time, so very long ago, different varieties of Salmon, in that order have come to the Squamish waters to help feed the people. And in the days of old, before the coming of the white people, the Indians obeyed the words of Chief Kos and were very careful to throw the salmon bones back into the water.

Halibut hook.

Halibut and Others

Halibut were regularly caught on U-or-V shaped hooks made of bent hemlock-root or yew wood attached, usually in pairs, one to each end of a slender rod, four or five feet (120 or 150 centimetres) long, with the main fishing line attached to its center.

The Coast Salish utilized a particularly interesting method for catching cod. They made a shuttlecock device which was lowered to the bottom on weights and then freed by means of a trip. The cod, fascinated by the whirling motion of the device, followed its rise to the surface and were speared by the waiting fishermen. Early white traders and settlers used to marvel at the deadly accuracy with which the Indians aimed their spears.

Giant sturgeon were taken from the Fraser and Squamish Rivers during spawning season. To locate the fish, the Indians used long-handled harpoons fitted with detachable heads to which were attached independent lanyards and floats. Once the position of the fish had been marked, further strikes could be made until the number of lines was sufficient to stand the strain of hauling the catch to the surface. The lines were made from dried kelp, which was of great strength after being stretched and treated, and could be found in single strands up to 150 feet in length.

Clam digger.

Shellfish

Shellfish have been a food of the Coastal tribes for thousands of years. The Indian women gathered them with their woven baskets, just as they gathered berries and dried them by the bushel for winter use.

Rock oysters, abalone, mussels, and even the barnacles found on the rocks at low tide, added to the supply of sea foods. But chief of all the shellfish was the clam, found in at least six varieties such as Rock clam, Razor clam, Bent nose, Butter clam, Cockle clam, and Horse clam. Clams have been a staple source of food supply for Coastal Indians from time immemorial. Along the beaches of the Northwest Coast, where Indian villages were located, there are great banks, sometimes running for miles, and containing stratum after stratum of clam shells, indicating century upon century of accumulation.

There is a legend that Raven, when he was a mischievous slave, stole the South Wind's daughter, thus forcing him to stop sending storms, for these storms drove the tide too far up the beach and the clams could not be uncovered.

Coast Salish women used open work baskets for clam gathering. This allowed the water to drip out, making the load lighter and easier to carry home.

The "clambake" style of steaming the clams is an Indian invention. The Coast Salish dug a hole in the ground, floored it with stones, and then built a fire on them. When the fire had burned out and the stones were thoroughly hot, the clams—still in their shells—were placed upon them and covered with earth or seaweed. The clams were allowed to steam in their own juice for an hour and by that time the shells had opened with the heat. The clams were then picked out and those which were not eaten immediately were impaled on skewers and hung in the sun to dry before being stored for winter use.

Clams were an important item of trade with inland people, the women eagerly trading good bags and baskets for them.

E.S. CURTIS

Sea Mammals

Bow hunter waits for seal to appear.

Unlike the Nootka and Makah, famed for their courageous exploits as whalers, the Coast Salish did not systematically hunt the huge mammals, which in any case were only rarely found in the straits. The Salish hunted smaller mammals, such as seals and porpoises, which were abundant and their flesh was greatly prized.

Hunting the mammals was the privilege of the higher ranks of Salish society. The hunt required superior nerve and skill and was regarded as a task involving much honor. The hunters bathed before they went out and engaged in religious preliminaries, sanctioning their proposed undertaking by the granting of spirit power to guide them on their dangerous mission.

The smaller sea mammals did not fight like a whale, and a three man canoe, with harpooner, float man and steersman, was all that was required for a successful hunt. The mammal was stabbed, and when tired was simply hauled in on the harpoon line and clubbed to death.

The heavy sea lion was a dangerous challenge and was the prey of only the more intrepid hunters. The meat of a seven hundred pound sea lion was sufficient to feed a whole village. The stomach could be used as a large bottle. The intestines, when twisted and dried, made tough and elastic bow strings.

Another method of hunting seals was to trap a herd on shore by means of large sinew nets, stretched between rocks at a point where the seals were in the habit of taking to the water. Many of the confused mammals were clubbed to death before the herd could make its escape in another direction.

45

Stellars Sea Lions in water and at rest.

Harbor seal.   Sea Otter.

Sea Otter

Legend has it that the sea otters were the richest of the magic people who lived under the sea. The handsome young chief of their village had come one day and courted an Indian maiden. He was dressed in soft and beautiful furs and she did not know who he was. When he took her in his arms and embraced her she felt wet and cold all over. Nevertheless, she married him and her family spread blankets like carpets under her feet as she walked down to the sea. She stepped into her canoe, which was piled with wedding gifts, and the shocked watchers saw the canoe suddenly pulled down out of sight beneath the waves. Later, she returned to the village with her baby, but she was turning into a sea otter. At last, the family advised her never to come again, as she had become more otter than woman.

The sea otters did indeed have something like a village in the sea. The females bore their young on rafts of kelp where they could be seen nursing their babies, playing and diving in the waves, sitting up to eat a sea urchin held in their forepaws or merely sleeping on their backs in the waves, their little forepaws folded across their breasts.

Sea otters, which are relatives of the mink and weasel, have fur so soft that the Indians called it by the word they later used to describe velvet. Wealthy indeed was the man who could afford to wear a mantle of the delicately luxurious sea otter fur. A man would trade two of his slaves for a single skin which could be cut up for use as a handsome head band or trimming, to enhance a mantle of cedar bark.

Yet in Indian days sea otter hunts were only occasional affairs. When White traders saw the commercial possibilities of sea otter pelts the unfortunate mammals were doomed. With skins selling in London for $300.00 a piece (an enormous sum in the 19th century) the Whites soon took over the hunting. They did not bother with canoes and harpoons but erected lookouts on the shore, on a tripod sixty feet high. The hunter (or otter murderer as he was known) sat there with a long range gun, like a miniature cannon, and shot at every furry head which appeared. Later he went out in his boat and gathered up the bodies. Today the sea otter after nearly three quarters of a century of extinction along the southern coast, has been re-introduced in smaller numbers from surviving stocks in Alaska. Hopefully this delightful animal will become common under strict protection.

Land Mammals

The Indians did not traditionally hunt young fawns or any animals not yet full grown. They believed that all animals must be allowed to grow and have young up to the height of their powers. Deer, elk, and bear meat were a welcome addition to the Coast Salish diet. But most of all the Indians wanted the skins. Elk skin was tough enough to turn an arrow and was often used as armor in battle. Deerskin was used as wrapping material for bundles carried in canoes or stored on shelves. Bearskins were large enough to wear as mantles, without any sewing involved. Sinews could be used for fastenings; bones were a necessity for pointed tools, and the teeth could be worn as ornamental jewelry or used as dice in gambling games.

Although a few brave men were trained to enter the deep forest and hunt, the Coast Salish hesitated to track game through a pathless wilderness of deadfalls and dense undergrowth.

Sometimes a deer or an elk would wander on to a beach near a coastal village. Then the people would band together to chase it into the water while a few of the men leaped hastily into canoes, armed with clubs or bows and arrows. While the unfortunate animal swam about, not knowing which way to turn, it was shot or clubbed to death. The Puget Sound people were especially fortunate with this method, for the Sound is full of islands and animals often swam to them from the mainland. Sometimes, old timers used to say, a deer would swim around to scare the ducks, just for fun! If this happened while the men were away, it did not deter the womenfolk. They would jump into the canoes, and armed only with their digging sticks, manage the kill by themselves!

But the usual method for capturing and killing large game was the use of traps. Traps have been used by man down through the ages, even when he had only sticks or clubs, and the trap is probably as old a device as the net.

Modern man thinks of the trap as a devilish device with steel teeth and a steel spring. The Indians used the natural spring in a strong young sapling, bent to the ground and ready to snap back when released. A noose would be tied to such a bent tree and arranged to lay on the ground among the leaves. The bent sapling would, of course, be standing close to a deer trail. When a deer happened to step in the noose, a triggering device was released,

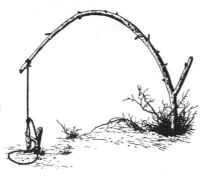

Spring trap used for bear and deer.

Dead falls used for bear and smaller fur-bearing mammals.

allowing the sapling to snap back, thus jerking the noose tightly around the animal's leg.

Another plan was to dig a pit in the trail and cover it lightly with sticks and leaves. These pits were perhaps fifteen feet across and so deep that any animal falling into one would suffer serious injury. Sometimes there was a double arrangement of a pit combined with a noose.

The brown or black bear, not so fierce as a grizzly, and living mostly on berries and spawning salmon, was also a frequent victim of ingenious Coast Salish trapping methods. The trapper baited the deadfall with a salmon tied with a string under a carefully balanced set of heavy logs. When the unfortunate bear jerked the salmon the heavy log, sometimes supporting the weight of other logs leaning against it, crashed down on him, injuring him severely or perhaps killing him outright.

Beavers, raccoons, cougars, bobcats, weasels, mink and rabbits—all were caught with the hunter's trap. The secret was to know the game paths used by the animals on their way to drink at some favorite pool or stream.

49

Black bear caught in dead fall.
Small coyote-like Salish dogs were used to
harass large game or drive it into water so
hunters could get close.

Salish Dogs

Little has been recorded about the Northwest Coast Indians' dogs. Seeing hunting dogs in Indian villages was certainly a surprise to early explorers, for such a sight was rare among any of the other Indian tribes in North America. According to the reports of early travelers, the dogs had the appearance of coyotes. They were highly trained by their masters, who called them by name, treated them like respected members of the family, and according to tales old Indians tell, even sang to them. The dogs were trained to enter the woods and chase the game out to the hunter. The Coast Salish used them particularly for driving mountain goats into ambush and for herding deer and elk into lakes, where they could be attacked and slain by men in canoes. What breed were these dogs? They have mixed long since with the pets of white settlers and reliable identification is no longer possible. Perhaps students interested in dog history will one day attempt to unravel the mystery of their origins.

Waterfowl

The Coast Salish knew the flyways along which flocks of mallard, teal, canvas back and other varieties of duck passed. The natives set up pairs of poles, perhaps forty feet high and between them they strung nets so fine as to be almost invisible to the naked eye. In the half light of dawn or twilight, the unwary birds flew straight into them, and the waiting Indians were there to wring their necks.

Sighting these net poles for the first time, the famous early explorer, Captain George Vancouver, mistook them for flagpoles, not realizing that the Indians did not raise flags.

Many other varieties of birds flew north over the skyways. Plovers came from the South Pacific; big white geese came down from the arctic to enjoy the mild winter. The Indians knew the habits and seasons for each and for each they had their traps and nets ready.

The birds' flesh was a welcome change from fish. The brightly feathered skins could be sewn together and worn as mantles, used as blankets, or worn as decorative finery.

Pacific Murres.

Seabirds

Sea birds, gulls and their eggs were also an important food resource. The offshore bird-nesting colonies were owned by individual bands and the birds and eggs harvested annually for their own use and as trade items.

Tufted puffins.

Cormorants.

Roots & Berries

Drying cakes of squashed red elderberries.　　　MUS. MAN. NAT. MUS. CAN.

With such a bountiful harvest of edible roots, bulbs, fruits, berries, green leaves and seaweed, provided by nature for the taking, the Coastal Indians watched with awe and dismay as the early settlers cleared the land and planted vegetable gardens which successfully grew corn, peas, carrots, onions, lettuce, cabbages, and other varieties of vegetables. To the Indians, this mass clearing, leaving nothing but bare earth, was an ugly desecration. To the Whites, arable untilled land was wasted land. Some of the settlers had endured hardships to come to this new land and gain the privilege of tilling the soil. They knew that one acre, sown to wheat and potatoes, would support as many people as twenty acres of hunting land. They neither knew nor cared that the fresh greens and berries, growing in such wild profusion, were as nourishing as the cultivated fare.

Yet, even for the Indians, food gathering could involve a lot of hard work. When the long winters were over and the first green shoots of horsetail rush, cow parsnip, black cap and salmonberry became edible, the natives—weary no doubt of their winter diet of dried food and fish oil—ate them raw, and some were so tender they needed no preparation. Others, such as salmonberry and cow parsnip, needed to have the outer bark stripped off.

The bulbs of the camas—a lily variety, relative of the onion, which spread its sky blue flowers abundantly over open, grassy areas—were much favored by the Coast Salish. They waited until August, when the flowers had gone to seed and the plants had shriveled, and then the women went out to dig the bulbs.

53

COOKING METHODS

Cooking methods among the Indians of the Northwest Coast were not dissimilar to those of the modern housewife: boiling, baking and broiling.

Broiling was the favored way of cooking fresh foods. The Coast Salish gathered a few green sticks with pointed ends. On these fresh fish or strips of meat could be propped before the embers of an outdoor fire and cooked to a turn. The Indians enjoyed meat and fish without salt.

Boiling was an indoor method, used in the cooking of dried foods in the long house during the winter months. Northwest Coast Indians had no metal pots and did not attempt to boil water over an open fire. The fire was used to heat stones, which were then dropped into a basket or wooden box containing cold water. As soon as the first stones cooled, they were removed and new ones added until the water boiled.

The baskets used as boiling pots were hard and tightly woven and when half filled with water they would not burn—unless the housewife, perhaps busy with her other cooking chores, forgot them and let the water boil out! Some of the old cooking baskets show scorched places on the bottoms, silent proof that the native cooks of early times also burned their pots.

Baking or steaming the food was an outdoor method of cooking which required a deep pit and might be described as an early Indian type of fireless cooker. A fire was lighted in a pit about three feet deep and rocks placed on top of the fuel. When the pit and the stones were thoroughly heated, the remnants of the fuel were removed and a specially chosen green herbage placed on the hot stones. The food was carefully placed on top of this with more green leaves added to give protection and moisture. The pit was then covered over with earth and hot embers and the food allowed to bake. The hard camas roots had to be baked in a pit of this sort for two or three days. A large roast of meat would cook in a few hours. Bundles of salmonberry shoots were ready in ten minutes. Steaming, instead of baking, was accomplished by punching a hole through the earth covering, and pouring a little water into the pit. The steaming process was especially satisfactory for cooking tough roots. The results were baked or steamed foods cooked to a tender succulence, with all the flavor and vitamin content preserved.

CRAFTS

Elaborate Salish basket work.

Basketry

Coast Salish women were famous for the high quality of their woven baskets, which were frequently adorned with beautifully imbricated designs. Each woman had three or four baskets, depending on the crops she wished to pick and the basket was her inseparable companion on her gathering trips. The women hung the baskets on their backs by means of a woven "tump line", which passed across their foreheads. For carrying clams the Coast Salish used open work baskets which would drain the salt water. For roots they might use the same but usually a basket with a slightly tighter weave was preferred. Tightly coiled baskets were used for berries, which are heavy when picked in quantity.

The Coast Salish women made their baskets during the long winter, but the tedious and time-consuming process of gathering and preparation of materials had to be done in the summertime, when the spruce and cedar roots and grasses were at their best. Roots and twigs had to be soaked, peeled and split, and grasses must be cured and sometimes dyed.

"When I begin to weave a basket," remarked one Indian lady, "My work is already half done."

Among the Coast Salish, the two main methods of basket-making involve weaving and coiling. In the woven baskets, the vertical warps were interlaced with more pliable wefts.

Depending upon final use, weaving methods were subject to considerable variation, with the woven basketry developing in twined and twilled forms. Twined work took the form of soft-rush bags and openwork, useful for carrying roots or clams and, on a larger scale, for the manufacturing of fish traps. Twilled products,

Tule gatherer. 1910 Puget
Sound

Salish basket-maker. Fine
coiled basket in foreground.

Fine quality baskets with imbrications of dark
cherry bark.

on the other hand, generally took the form of pouches, sewing-baskets, or hold-alls.

The heavy coiled baskets were known as "hard baskets" and were woven by an entirely different method. In this method the foundation strands go around the basket, not up and down. They are coiled around in a spiral, and each is sewn to the one below it by means of vertical stitches, passing over the upper strand and under or through the lower. Bone awls were used as needles and the stitching was of threads of roots or grass. The part of the coil being sewn was pressed together with the fingers while the binding strand was pulled tight with the teeth. So tightly were these baskets sewn that when swollen by soaking they were completely watertight.

Decorating the coiled baskets was done by a clever process termed imbrication. Bear grass was the favored decorating material but it was fragile as straw and used alone could not have held a basket together. Strips of this glossy grass, or dyed bark, were overlapped upon the overcast stitching which binds the coils of the "hard basket" together. A row of it, pleated under the sewing stitches around a basket, looked something like a row of shingles, overlapping at the side instead of the top and bottom. One of the most common and best loved designs was done in deep Vs and is believed by some women to represent the waves in a lake, the idea for the design having in ancient times come to a basket weaver in the form of a vision. Another popular design was a series of diagonal lines, zigzagging around the basket in harmonious forms which some Indians say were originally inspired by lightning storms.

The art of weaving the coiled basket is slowly dying out among the Coast Salish. The older baskets, still beautiful and with age adding a soft patina to the imbrication, are much sought after as historic works of art by the museums and by collectors who admire them for the sheer artistry of weave and design.

58

Weaving

Spinning goats wool.   B.C. PROV. MUS.

Coast Salish women, utilizing a simple loom, wove in wool—a practise uncommon in North America since the continent was not well-supplied with wool-bearing animals until after the introduction of sheep by white men. In addition, the Puget Sound women had their own little wool-bearing animal—a tame dog, quite small, but with a thick coat of creamy wool which could be shorn at regular intervals. When the wool was hacked off with a mussel shell knife, the fleece was so thick that according to one historian you could lift it up by one corner, like a mat. The Coast Salish also utilized the wool of the mountain goat. The Salish Indians along the Fraser River sometimes hunted the goats and traded the hides to the Coast. They also searched over the hillsides in spring and summer, when the goats were shedding, and gathered the tufts of fur which rubbed off on the bushes as the animals passed by. Perhaps it was this gift of wool which inspired Salish women to begin weaving cloth.

Early explorers describe the dogs as having the appearance of Pomeranians, usually white in color, but sometimes varying to a brownish black. They were usually kept on tiny islands in Puget Sound and the Straits of Juan de Fuca and were not found among the more northerly Indians of the Northwest Coast.

The women would paddle out daily from the village with food and drink for the dogs and always took them along with them during prolonged absences from the village on food gathering trips and other necessary excursions.

A woman's wealth was said to have been judged by the number of dogs she owned.

59

Paul Kane painting of old Salish two-bar loom, showing wool dog.

Salish weavers at Chilliwack have recently revised old Salish tradition and are now producing first class pieces of art.

Salish loom at Esquimalt.

Captain George Vancouver reported meeting a group of two hundred Indians, most of them in canoes, but a few walking along with a drove of about forty dogs, which were sheared close to the skin like sheep.

Coast Salish weavers mixed the dog wool with that of the mountain goat, and even with goose down and the fluff of the fireweed plant.

The opening of the Hudson's Bay trading posts and the subsequent appearance of the easily obtainable Hudson's Bay blankets spelled the death knell for the weaving of these beautiful Salish blankets and mantles, only a few of which survive today in museums and private collections.

With the coming of the gold rush in 1858 and the resultant drastic changes in Coast Salish life styles, the dogs were no longer a valuable commodity and soon became extinct. Today there is not an Indian living who even remembers how they looked.

The wool of the dogs was much finer than that of the goats, and the yarns produced from it are very much like those of a fine grade, commercial wool. The shearing was sometimes repeated two or three times in a summer and even then it was hard to get wool enough for many blankets. Women would mix the dog wool with mountain goat wool and together with goose or duck down and the cotton from the fireweed and other plants, in any proportions available. Clay beaten into the wool with a flat, sword-like piece of wood helped remove the grease from the wool and also whitened it, for dog wool was not so white as the wool of the mountain goat. Next the weaver combed the fibers out with her fingers or hand carders and then rolled them on her leg. The wool was then ready for spinning. The spindle used was a smooth stick three of four feet long. At its lower end was the whorl of carved wood (often beautifully decorated), to keep the strands from slipping.

The loom for weaving the yarn consisted of two horizontal rollers supported in slots cut in wooden uprights set in the ground. Although not always used, the alternate strands of the warp were often kept apart by a simple heddle of thin wood to allow the hand

61

IAN McKAIN

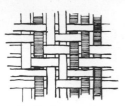

Twilled weave.

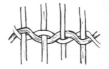

Twined weave.

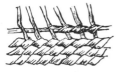

Wrapped twining.

Mrs. Jean Albin learning weaving techniques from Chilliwack master weaver, Mrs. James.

to pass through. The warp was run around these rollers in a series of continuous cords so that the web could frequently be pulled around to a convenient position for the weaver, who always wove from the top downwards.

The technique used in weaving the goat wool blanket could be compared to that of twilled basketry, in which the weft crosses the warp in the sequence of over two and under one.

There was little use of color until the White people brought yarn in trade. Then a few really beautiful blankets were made in fine yarn and magnificent color. With the arrival of the ready-made and easy-to-get Hudson's Bay blankets, the art of the Salish weaver was given up and soon died out altogether. Some of these beautiful blankets were ten or twelve feet long and were used for bedding. Smaller ones—perhaps half the length—were used as mantles.

Thanks mostly to the efforts of the late Oliver Wells, the art of weaving the Coast Salish blanket has recently enjoyed a sudden and dramatic revival. Talented Salish women are weaving their blankets again on simple looms, just as they did more than a century ago. Beautiful natural dyes color the blankets with attractive geometric patterns. Alder bark can be used for red; lichen for yellow; cedar and hemlock bark for brown; Oregon grape for a yellow-green and copper for blue-green.

62

Simplified Salish patterns.

Salish tribes on southern Vancouver Island, and more recently on the mainland, have applied knitting techniques learned from Scottish settlers, to specialized sweaters and garments.

CANOES

Salish hunting canoe.

Travel among the Indian tribes of the Northwest was essentially by sea or via the inland waterways. The canoe was the Indians' only means of transportation over long distances. Without it they would have been penned up in their villages, with no way to visit, hunt, trade, or go to war.

The famous yet frail birchbark canoes of other North American Indian tribes would have been of little use to Northwest Coast Indians in rough Pacific waters. Instead they crafted sturdy dugouts from the trunk of the cedar, sometimes fifty feet long and six to eight feet wide. The famous explorers, Lewis and Clark, reported that the largest ones could "carry eight to ten thousand pounds, or twenty to thirty persons."

The Coast Salish did not traditionally build great ocean going canoes although they were known to have traded furs for them with the Nootka on Vancouver Island. Most seaworthy of all, and certainly most beautiful in form and line, were the Haida canoes, with their projecting bows and sterns raised high above the water.

In early times some canoes had sails made of cedarbark matting. The origins of these sails is not known. Some say the idea came from White traders but the use of sails could have arrived long ago—perhaps with the sighting of a Chinese junk, wrecked in Pacific waters.

Northern style open-sea Kwakuitl canoes, sometimes purchased in trade by Salish.

E.S. CURTIS

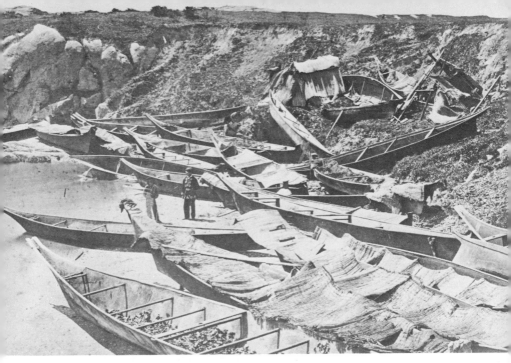

Salish canoes near Victoria about 1900.

Dugout canoes were made in various shapes and sizes according to their purpose. Apart from the great sea-going canoes, there were inland varieties—shorter and shallower freight canoes for rivers, small hunting canoes about ten feet long and a one man canoe used mainly for duck hunting. Then there was a kind of knock-about canoe used for sealing and, in modern times, the slim slick ones for racing.

A common sight at an Indian village, especially one near salt water, were the many dugouts of various shapes and sizes, drawn up and turned over on the beach and covered with mats to protect them from the sun.

Canoe builders were honored in Coast Salish villages and there were generally only one or two such craftsmen in each village. The manufacturing of the canoe was originally the work of this specialist who was assisted by spirit helpers. Because of this belief, special rites were conducted, songs were sung and taboos observed by the builder and his wife during the period of construction. This privacy was especially insisted upon during the more critical phases, such as the first splitting of the log and the steaming and spreading of the sides.

The log had not only to be hollowed out but must also be

65

shaped and curved. For this the canoe maker used what might almost be described as cooking methods! A fire was lighted around the outside of the canoe at a distance which would heat the wood without scorching it. The canoe, roughly shaped and hollowed out by means of splitting off slabs with wedges, was then almost filled with water which was heated with hot stones. It is at this point that the skill and experience of the canoe-maker was put to its greatest test. When the canoe was first hollowed out, the bottom was deliberately left bellied up in the center, and a similar line allowed to the gunwales. This form allowed for spreading, a process which could add as much as two feet to the original width of the log. Thus a log three feet in width might become a canoe with a five foot beam. Between the warm fire and the steaming process, the wood fibers became soft and pliable. The worker meanwhile cut stout pieces of yew wood, just the width the canoe would have at various points along its length. At the center, of course, it would be considerably wider than the original log, while it would taper at both ends. The sticks of yew wood were wedged between the gunwales, like thwarts, so that the sides were kept bulging. Then the water was dipped out and the canoe allowed to dry in its curved shape. The fine work was done by patient charring with fire, controlled by damp sand, and then hacking off the charcoal with an adze. The D-adze was used for the final shaping and even finer work was done with chisels held in elk-horn handles. Surface areas were further sanded by rubbing with the rough part of a dogfish skin.

Indian fishing dugouts. Songhees Reserve, Victoria.

Coast Salish fishermen on Quinault River.

Modern sleek Salish racing canoes.

The Indians of the Coastal North often painted their canoes with exciting designs representing creatures of the sea such as killer whales or sharks and even birds and animals. Among the more southerly tribes, paint was sparse and only two colors were utilized. The inside of the canoe was usually colored red. The Indians made a sort of oil paint by mixing red ochre with fish or seal oil, just as modern paint is mixed with linseed oil. The outside of the canoe was first smoothed with shark skin and then charred lightly with a cedar-bark torch. This singed off the roughnesses and left it a dull black.

The thwarts were fastened tightly to the sides of the canoe by cedar withes, passed through holes in thwart and gunwale. Paddlers had to sit or kneel or lean against them and since they were round poles, they were never very comfortable unless cedar-bark mats were folded over them as a kind of padding.

Paddles were carved from yew or maple wood and polished smooth with sharkskin. Some paddles were pointed at the end so they could be dug into the beach to hold the canoe but usually the paddle blade had a rounded end.

Raiding party returning to Salish village on Vancouver Island.   67

RELIGION

Shaman salmon rattle.

Among the Coast Salish, as indeed with all of the Northwest Coast tribes, almost every action in life centered around Spirit Power. Animals, birds, rocks, trees, fish—in fact all objects, whether animate or inanimate—contained spirits which could influence the Indians' life.

Therefore, since the native deeply felt the influence of the unseen world in every happening, he had to constantly strive to positively influence these spirits on his behalf. Yet there was no ritualistic worship of a Supreme Being. When the White people came and tried to wipe out native beliefs and Christianize the Indians, they had no understanding of how deeply they were reaching into Indian moral codes and behavioral patterns. There was a mistaken belief among early missionaries that native carvings representing family crests on totem poles or welcoming figures, etc., in the form of animals, birds, sea mammals, were worshipped in some form of pagan idolatry.

The Coast Salish lived in their little world—filled with many spirit forms, guardian spirits, supernatural beings, transformers, and demi-gods endowed with various powers and jurisdictions. As with other Coastal groups there was a suggestion of a "Creator of the World" but his powers do not appear to have been absolute and because of this lack of total omnipotence he frequently required aid from near equals who enjoyed concurrent jurisdiction in some fields.

Christians believe that the force of life is concentrated in one God, all pervasive, yet residing in the heavens. The Coast Salish, like most North American Indians, were more inclined to think of life's force as pervading the world like an electric current. This power might show itself in almost anything, from the cry of the loon to a flash of lightning. There existed an underlying belief in the essential oneness of man with nature. Originally, according to Indian belief, all living creatures shared in a world of mutual harmony and understanding. One must at all times preserve a proper respect for the habits and dwelling places of all species of life. This "oneness of life philosophy" led to the concept of "animal people"—beings with the characteristics of both animals and man. Strip a bird of his feathers, or the fur from a bear, or the scales from a fish and the form becomes indistinguishable from human form. Thus a deserving man might establish a close relationship with a wolf spirit who would become his "helper" and aid him in developing wolf power to assist him in growing to be a great hunter.

The Coast Salish believed that the soul of a man was twofold. First and foremost was that indestructible spark, which, once departed went to the sunset, where it remained forever. That which was left behind was the earthly body and its shadows—these shadows held a three-part existence and remained on the earthly scene with either good or evil intent, depending on the character of the person in life.

Temporary Indian encampment at Mission for a "big religious event in summer of 1888."

MUS. MAN. NAT. MUS. CAN.

Shaman charm of bone.

MUS. MAN. NAT. MUS. CAN.

Shaman or
Medicine Man

The Shaman was a very important man in his community. He was the Medicine Man, the Indian equivalent of the modern doctor. Moreover, he played a leading part in all ceremonial functions and was much sought after for his help and advice in times of trouble and distress.

Early missionaries painted an unpleasant and untrue picture of the Medicine Man as a charlatan and a cheat. On the contrary, a Shaman had a sincere belief in himself and often affected remarkable cures among his people. Perhaps he practised a form of hypnotism, or used the power of suggestion, on his patients, but among the Indians at least there persisted a firm belief in his powers and in his ability to cure people of sickness and suffering.

Among the Coast Salish there were two classes of Shamans— those who held supreme powers in the arts of clairvoyance, the curing of the sick and the controlling of the ghosts and shadows of men, and those of lesser powers who concerned themselves with minor illnesses and the warding off of adverse influences. The latter were usually women, who applied themselves mostly to the practise of midwifery.

The Shaman was required to lead an exemplary life among his people. He was repeatedly required to give demonstrations of his powers before being accepted as a Medicine Man who could accept fees for his work. He had an animal "helper" who had been revealed to him in a dream during his days as a novice and this animal became his relative and could be invoked by him at any time when assistance was needed.

The Coast Salish believed that disease originated as an evil

70

Rattle by Floyd Joseph

spirit which had penetrated the body and induced pain and suffering. The Shaman, performing ritualistic songs and dances and sprinkling water over the patient, attempted to draw out the evil spirit by sucking on the afflicted part. Proof of his success depended on the patient's recovery. If the sick person failed to get better a feeling of enmity could develop toward the Medicine Man whose powers had failed him.

The Shamans attempted to keep up their prestige by staging public exhibitions. At many of the big feasts there were doctor contests, where Shamans removed snakes from their bodies, or picked hot stones out of the fire and danced with them.

The life of the Shaman was full of dangerous suspicions and intrigues. If too many of his patients died, the entire village might begin to fear him and conclude he was a sorcerer, with the result that someone could decide to go out and kill him as a public service.

A missionary who once witnessed a Medicine Man at work wrote later that he never forgot the occasion. The patient lay in a coma on rush mats inside the long house. The Shaman had first to make a diagnosis. He went into a spirit dance calling on his spirit helper to help him "see" what was afflicting the sick man. Everyone in the village had gathered to beat on the roof with poles to help him achieve his power. The Medicine Man, masked and wearing a head-dress of cedarbark and shaking his rattle, bounded in and danced around the patient. His helpers followed him, repeating a song, until finally the Shaman went into a trance, showing that his spirit was with him. When he came out of it, weary and exhausted, he had full knowledge of what was causing the patient's ailment.

Medicine Men were not known to get particularly rich. Why did some men choose to go through the grueling rituals of obtaining Medicine Power? The answer lies in the prestige the Shaman enjoyed. He was something like a priest and elder statesman in his village. He was consulted on almost every occasion and commanded more obedience than the Chief of the village. He was feared as well as respected and his prominence in the village was forever assured.

71

Secret Societies

Secret societies among the Coast Salish were neither as numerous nor as well-organized as those of the northern tribes. It seems likely that such societies were largely the result of a culture transfer. For example, there was a variety of such societies existing among Coast Salish bands in close contact with the Kwakiutl. Yet farther south, in the Puget Sound and Fraser River area, secret societies were scarce and not highly regarded.

The function of these societies was basically religious. Yet the wildly mysterious initiation ceremonies seemed utterly pagan to early White missionaries and under the influence of the Church the societies were either carried on in great secrecy, or died out altogether.

The spirit which inspired the society was always wild and terrifying. Usually it was some sort of cannibal monster which most tribes referred to as "black tamanous" (tah-mah-no-us) or black spirit. One could not hope to receive this spirit by merely seeking it. The initiate must also pay high dues to the society and then be prepared to give a huge feast. This meant that only rich men's sons could join, and the society had only a few members in any one tribe. Nevertheless, a member's prestige was very high. They could, it was whispered, stand any kind of pain without feeling it. They looked so terrifying in their costumes that people obeyed them out of fear.

Initiation played an important part and novices were required to be of pure mind and unimpeachable behavior. As a consequence, most of the novices were adolescents, with their fathers acting as sponsors. When the probationer was granted entry into the society, he traditionally disappeared into the woods where he fasted, bathed frequently in cold water and scrubbed himself with rough cedar bark boughs. The combination of extreme physiological deprivation and psychological preparation eventually brought about a successful outcome to the vision quest. During the initiate's absence, his mother worked new mountain-goat wool blankets for him and perhaps ornaments of cedar bark. Then when the youth returned, his father gave a five-day feast. During the feast, dances were performed, to which all people were admitted. The society members occupied one side of the long house. Dressed in their regalia of cedar bark ornaments, their faces blackened to emphasize the solemnity of the occasion, and their hair strewn with down to

Secret society Skhway-Khwey dancer and mask.

indicate inward rejoicing, the members were a truly impressive sight. At the end of the five days, the novice underwent a ceremonial bathing in the sea and again retired to the woods for further experience of privation and exposure, returning only from time to time for instruction in the rites of the society. This woods-dwelling period was finally terminated by the black spirit revealing itself to the youth and becoming his guard and guiding him in all his future ways.

Having found his spirit the novice returned triumphantly to the house where another feast, accompanied by a Potlatch, was given. The time had now come for the graduate to perform his dance and reveal himself to the people as a full-fledged member of the secret society.

Most of the animal masks used by the Coast Salish on these occasions are not native to them but are borrowed from other tribes. One mask, however, which is truly Coast Salish in origin, is the remarkable Skhway Khwey mask which is used in the Nanaimo and Cowichan area and the adjacent mainland in ceremonial dances to this day.

Digging Sticks

Digging roots.

Digging sticks.

Breaking sod with nothing but a pointed stick could be back-breaking work. The sticks or tools for digging were usually made of tough spruce wood with carved and pointed ends. The sticks for digging shellfish were scooped, with pointed ends to facilitate the digging, whereas the sticks for roots were even less elaborate, with a slightly curved and pointed end and a simple handle for gripping.

In the case of the camas lily they dug a trench around an entire clump of plants and then took up the whole thing, shaking the earth back into the hole and placing the bulb roots in the carrying basket.

MYTHS AND LEGENDS

The Coast Salish, along with other Indian tribes, had no written language and therefore stories of tribal origin, history, achievements and newly learned facts had to be passed on verbally from one generation to the next through myths and legends.

Many Coast Salish myths are found among the legends of the inland plateau people—the ancestral homeland of Coast Salish. For example, the "Creation" myth of the Interior which tells of an Old Man who walked the earth creating the outstanding features of the landscape, or altering conditions previously established by supernatural "Transformers" such as the Raven and Coyote, has many variations among coastal tribes.

Cowichan dance house by Mildred Valley Thornton.

Story telling was an essential part of the cultural heritage of the Indian. Gathered around the lodge fires during the long winter evenings, children listened to legends and myths reaching far back in Coast Salish history and young minds became a storehouse of knowledge. The stories were acted out with intense dramatic effect with the speaker waving his arms, crouching, and even changing his voice in dramatic imitations of the characters involved in his story.

Legends and myths also formed the basis for the ceremonial songs and spirit dances which took place inside the long houses when the people gathered together for the winter ceremonies.

Sea lion and First Man, who is dressed in traditional Coast Salish costume, from the painting by Floyd Joseph. Floyd's inspiration for the painting inspired by the ancient Squamish legend of the First Man as told by the late Dominic Charlie.

Quamichan potlatch, 1900.

POTLATCH

The very cornerstone of Coast Salish society was based on the potlatch, as indeed it was with all of the Northwest Coast tribes. The Potlatch was a rather complicated "giving away" or redistribution of wealth ceremony, in which the recipients of lavish gifts were bound to reciprocate by inviting the donors to a return Potlatch, where they must prove their standing and influence by giving back far more than they had received. These endless Potlatches, and the fantastic ceremonial rituals that were so much a part of it all, fed and encouraged the natural creative urges of the native people.

Many events could be the excuse for the giving of a Potlatch—the building of a new long house, the raising of a Mortuary Pole, the birth of a baby, the coming of age of a daughter or a nephew, a marriage, succession to a leading position in the village, or the taking of new and more honorable names. Sometimes a Potlatch was given to celebrate several events at the same time. When the Potlatch was banned by the government because of its impoverishing effects, the blow struck deep into the structure of Northwest Coast society.

76   **Preparations for potlatch at Quamichan.**

The three children and photo of a fourth represent members of the family who have died.
The blankets and other gifts are now being distributed to the masses who have come to share death commemoration potlatch.

LIFE AND DEATH

Before the advent of the White man and the days of the Indian reservations—when the native people were frequently forced to abandon their villages and move to land set aside for them by the Government—life's pace was a slow and leisurely affair, with time being measured in moons and seasons, rather than in minutes and hours and the days of the calendar month.

Most of the village sites were established on low benches, just above the high-water level of the sea, or above the flood level of the rivers. With the help of early photographs we can picture the long houses, with their lean-to roofs and plank sides, the large array of canoes pulled up on the beaches, sometimes turned over and covered with rush mats to protect them from the sun, and the great piles of empty clam shells, plus a certain amount of miscellaneous rubbish including kelp-ends and other refuse.

Inside a long house we might see a woman using the Northwestern spindle, in order to produce a two-ply yarn. Another woman might be sitting at her loom, busily weaving a blanket, with her baby nearby, snugly suspended in his cradle. On the floor, near one of the smoldering lodge fires, is an assortment of wooden cooking boxes and woven baskets along with a number of smooth round stones, which have been collected as being just the right size and shape for use in heating water for cooking. Several men, with no immediate outside duties, loll near the fires, and children at play run in and out of the long house.

Village scenes indicated a settled communal existence with all of life's basic necessities easily obtainable without too much effort or exertion.

At different seasons the villages fairly hummed with activity, such as when the salmon were running. Fish had to be caught, dried and stored. Oil had to be extracted from the eulachons and salmon heads to be rendered down. Also in season, there were clams to be dug and cooked, roots and bulbs to be found, and berries to be gathered.

But during the winter months there were periods of extended leisure and it was during these cold weather months that most of the games, dances and other ceremonies and festivities took place.

Quamichan village, 1866.

Coast Salish graves of "People who have gone to the land of the dead." Prior to the coming of the White man, the funeral involved a complicated ritual. The face of the deceased was painted red and black. His body, usually in a crouching position with the hands around the knees, was placed in a box which was raised about five feet from the ground. The box was then placed in a high tree, in canoes on isolated islands or along parts of the shore where permanent cemeteries were established. When the White man came and the new authority under the Christian church was established the ancient Indian burial practises ceased and the bodies were interred beneath the ground. In these interesting old photographs we see Coast Salish graves, with carved Memorial figures, as they looked around the turn of the century.

Coast Salish Graves

THE DORMANT PERIOD

Family on Fraser River taking time from cutting wood.

The Coast Salish, living as they did around the beaches and the waterways of some of the most desirable land in the Province of British Columbia and the State of Washington, were among the first of the Northwest Coast Indians to have their lives disrupted by the infiltration of non-Indians into their territory. That infiltration soon became a veritable tide, beginning with the Gold Rush days of the 1850's. When white settlements such as Victoria, New Westminster, Vancouver and Seattle grew and expanded into Coast Salish territory, the native inhabitants of their ancestral villages were abruptly moved on the government supervised Reservation land. Only the Indians themselves could really understand the heartbreak of those early days when they were forced to accept a new religion and fit themselves into a life style which was totally foreign and distasteful to them.

The Indians soon found they could no longer roam the land at will, hunting and fishing in what had formerly been their own territorial regions. Some of the best berry picking and root gathering areas had suddenly become private property, owned by Whites. When the government banned the Potlatch and took away the authorities of the Chiefs and Nobles of the villages and the

Gathering for Sunday band concert.

missionaries halted the practise of Shamanism, the final blow had been delivered, and Indian cultures collapsed in a state of chaotic disintegration.

The Coast Salish lived under a rigid caste system and according to early writers there were four classes evident in Coast Salish society—the princely class, the nobles, the commoners, and the slaves. When this caste system disintregated under the new order of things brought about by White domination, the Coast Salish found themselves disembodied, as it were, from their own cultural traditions. Once proud Chiefs and Nobles, shorn of most of their former prestige and authority, wandered about on the new Reservations "like fallen Eagles", according to one missionary observer.

There was no actual war between Indian and White in British

81

Columbia, although British gunboats went up and down the coast, firing on Indian villages when Governor Sir James Douglas faced some dissidence and found it necessary to cement and implement the new authority.

Further south, among the Coast Salish in the State of Washington, an actual war erupted, and the Puyallup and Nisqually bands, backed up by the Duwamish and Klikitat, attacked the town of Seattle—then a mere collection of wooden buildings. The Puyallup and Nisqually had good reason for the attack. Their land had been right in the middle of the White settlements. Instead of being allowed to learn to farm there, with the help of tools and education, they were moved to a gravel bluff, with no water, no fertile land, and no pasture. The Nisqually could not farm and they found themselves literally starving, and the situation among the Puyallup was little better.

Historians say the Indians might have taken Seattle if there had not been a warship in the harbor. Yet it was never the traditional policy of Northwest Coast Indians to occupy land other than their own. A sudden attack, a few killings, the taking of slaves, and a quick retreat with as little loss as possible was the only type of war waged in Indian days. In the attack on Seattle, the Indians burned two houses, shot two men and drove off the cattle. This small war took place in the winter of 1855-56 and the attack on Seattle, which the Indians at first regarded as a victory that might hopefully scare the White man away, resulted in a wholesale disaster for them. Leschi, the leader of the Nisqually, was hanged. He had led 200 Indians against 600 fighters on the White side, including the troopers. The Indians, with no home base, were camped in the swamps at the base of the Cascade mountains. They died like flies from starvation and finally Leschi led the gaunt men and women and dying children up over the mountain ice and back into the coastal plain. There they surrendered, Leschi was hanged, and the last embers of Indian resistance died away.

The years 1850 to 1860 marked the beginnings of a long cultural sleep for the Coast Salish. Some left their Reservations and camped as near as they could get to their old villages, eking out a living by fishing, gathering clams, roots and berries and selling whatever they could to White settlers. They even traded their beautifully woven baskets, now mere curios in the new order of things, in exchange for cast off clothing and a little money.

REBIRTH OF ART AND CULTURE

Painting of Chief Mathias Joe Capilano
by Mildred Valley Thornton.

The 1920s were probably the lowest years in the cultural history of the Northwest Indians. By 1930 the Coast Salish had almost abandoned their traditional ceremonial costumes in favor of the buckskins and feathered headdresses of the Prairie Indians, who remain the stereotype of the non-Indian's image of the noble aboriginal of long ago.

The legendary Coast Salish hats, conical in shape and made of human hair adorned at the crown with two duck or loon feathers, were replaced with a colorful but non-traditional headdress of eagle feathers (or whatever feathers were available).

Robes of otter and bearskin, lynx or marten, blankets of creamy wool, and glistening capes of duck or loon feathers gave way to the fringed and beaded buckskins of the Prairie Indians.

But in recent years, the Coast Salish, like other Indian tribes of the Northwest Coast, have felt the restless stirrings of a new pride in their cultural heritage. Such venerable Chiefs and Nobles as the late Chief August Jack Khatsahlano, who was the last of forty great Medicine Men or Shamans of the ancient Order of Dancers of the Squamish Indians, and that grand old Chiefteness of the Squamish band, Mary Capilano, whose Indian name was Lay-hu-lette, (which means "the beginning of the world") continued to cling to the old beliefs and customs and to exert a powerful influence among their people.

The late Chief Mathias Joe, and that fabulous interpreter of Coast Salish dances, the late Dominic Charlie were—among a mere handful of their contemporaries—also instrumental in helping to maintain a link with the colorful past.

83

Comox welcoming pole, 1879.   Early Quamichan outside house post.

Yet it is on the shoulders of the young Indians of the present generation, who balance the nostalgia engendered by their elders' storied dreams of a return to the old ways with their own exciting vistas of things to come, that the future rests.

Significant of Coast Salish aspirations is the renaissance of Coast Salish art, which has been gathering momentum for the last quarter of a century. The art of the Coast Salish has been described as a direct art, with Coast Salish carvers of the pre-white era showing little understanding of the decorative, two-dimensional art of the northern coastal tribes. Carved house-posts, grave figures, and ceremonial dance masks were usually plainly carved and simply designed with a sparing use of paint, yet much of the work revealed a stark beauty and emanated a power which lifted it to comparable levels with the best in Northwest Coast art. In addition many of the old Coast Salish masks, notably the legendary Skhway Khwey mask—a much revered mask used in the Secret Society dances—compared favorably with the sophisticated northern style masks of other Northwest Coast tribes. Deeply carved, and richly designed and painted, these masks are jealously guarded by their owners, and the history of the Skhway Khwey mask is deeply rooted in Coast Salish art and culture. Today they are rarely made and continue to be much coveted by collectors of west coast native art.

Comox village, 1867-70.

   With the collapse of Indian cultures under the White influence, Coast Salish art—like that of all the Northwest Coast tribes—languished for many years, until it almost reached the point of extinction. Coast Salish artists began carving small "tourist totems" (some of which had real merit) for sale in gift shops, but the art had little direction or meaning, and the people remained heavily under the influence of the church and white officialdom.

   Gradually, over the years, the attitude of white people toward their Indian brothers underwent a profound change and a new interest was kindled in Indian art. It probably began with the recognition, in the late 1920s, of the work of artist Emily Carr. Miss Carr had traveled extensively for many years among the native people of British Columbia, painting Indian villages and totem poles. The wild beauty and power of Northwest Coast native carvings was dramatically captured and faithfully portrayed in the hundreds of water colors and oils this courageous and talented woman left as a legacy to all Canadians.

   With their once decimated populations on the upswing and the Potlatch again legalized by a benevolent and newly enlightened federal government, new incentives to re-establish their art and culture have grown rapidly among the Coast Salish.

   Much credit for his contribution toward keeping Coast Salish art alive as a moving, growing force must be given to Simon Charlie, a member of the Cowichan Indian band. Simon was born at Koksilah, a few miles south of Duncan, on Vancouver Island, on November 15, 1919. Charlie's vigorously direct and powerfully carved totem poles, portraying Cowichan legends of Thunderbird, Spirit Dancer, Bear, Killer Whale and Frog can be found in Museums and Galleries right across the North American continent. One of his greatest works, a Cowichan Indian Welcoming figure, stands inside the main doors of the Provincial Museum in Victoria, welcoming visitors to the Museum. In times past, such a figure, which is that of a man with his arms raised in a welcoming salute, might stand on a beach to welcome guests attending a Potlatch.

Modern day Coast Salish art is changing and has moved closer to the stylized designs of the north. The work of Floyd Joseph, a brilliant young artist and carver whose art bears the stamp of genius quality, is significantly representative of this trend. Floyd, a member of the Squamish band of the Coast Salish, was born on the Capilano Reserve in North Vancouver, on October 29, 1953. From early childhood Floyd had demonstrated a remarkable ability to draw and paint. As he grew older his creative qualities became increasingly apparent and he discovered his ability to carve.

Floyd completed grades 11 and 12 at the Carson Graham High School in North Vancouver and while there he was inspired by the work of Frank Perry. European trained and a friend of the outstanding Haida Indian artist and master-carver Bill Reid, Perry is a superb artist and sculptor in his own right.

"He (Perry) had a very profound influence over me," recalls Floyd. "He not only inspired me to greater heights as an artist, but he taught me to be self-confident and self-reliant and made me realize the importance of personal independence."

Even in those early days, when he was not yet out of his teens, Floyd's carved and painted masks, bowls, plaques and totem poles held unusual originality and charm and were eagerly sought by art lovers from all walks of life.

Today, at age twenty-four, Floyd's art reveals a maturity far beyond his years. His sculptured wood carvings are amazingly life-like and beautiful. His carved Eagles, Loons, Ravens, Bears, Whales, and other creatures relevant to Coast Salish legends are delicate to the point of extreme fragility. The painted designs that complement and adorn them are fincly balanced and reminiscent of the classic form lines associated with the northern art styles of the

Doug La Fortune   **Floyd Joseph**

Tsimshian Indians, whose exquisite human face masks and carved animal forms contain a tender sensitivity rarely equalled in Northwest Coast art.

Brothers Doug and Tom LaFortune, David Nahanee, Cicero August, John Joseph, and Johnny and Delmar Joseph and Ronnie George, and Johnny and Tyrone Joseph, are but a few of the modern day Coast Salish artists whose work has contributed significantly in the furthering of Coast Salish cultural aspirations.

Beaver-thunderbird pole by Doug La Fortune

Dancer

Thunderbird pole

SIMON CHARLIE CARVINGS

Simon Charlie of Koksilah is one of the
master carvers who restimulated interest
in traditional Coast Salish carving.

His bold images reflect the traditional
figurine quality of Salish art.

Frog-bear-man-serpent pole.